Alfred's Kid's Drum Course 1

(Element

The Easiest Drum Method Ever!

Dave Black • Steve Houghton

Cover and interior illustrations by Jeff Shelly.
Interior photos courtesy of Remo, Inc.

Alfred

Copyright © 2004 by Alfred Publishing Co., Inc.
All rights reserved.   Printed in USA.
ISBN 0-7390-3609-2 (Book and CD)

Contents

Preface

Everyone can gain great satisfaction from listening to and playing musical instruments. Almost everything around us, including our bodies, can be used as a sound source. Discovering musical sounds with everyday objects can be both fun and rewarding.

A number of musical sounds can be produced with simple, inexpensive objects found around the home. Many of these non-traditional instruments (such as pots and pans, bowls, and cardboard boxes) can be tuned to a variety of pitches by the use of finger pressure. Like traditional instruments, these objects can be used with parents and other family members in the home for personal enjoyment or in the classroom by teachers interested in stimulating creative ideas for their students. All these items can be great tools in the study of both sound and rhythm awareness.

Acknowledgments

The authors wish to thank Karen Farnum Surmani, Jodi Malone, Kate Westin, Tom Ryan, Kathy Spiro, Kathy Bartling, Sharon Munson, Greg Plumblee, Chalo Eduardo and Sandy Lindgren for their invaluable assistance in the writing of this book. A very special thanks to Todd Schroeder for his engineering, orchestrations, and multi-keyboard talents.

Selecting Your Sound Source

A *sound source* is anything used to create musical sound. Traditional instruments, such as drums, are the most commonly used sound sources, but other objects can be used as sound sources as well. Non-traditional instruments include everyday objects that can be found at home or made in the classroom, as well as a variety of manufactured items designed with fun and creativity in mind. Below is a partial list of recommended sound sources to help get you started.

Non-Traditional Instruments

Remo Sound Shapes Played with beaters, sticks or mallets.

Practice Pad Mounted on a stand or placed on a flat surface and played with sticks or beaters.

Boomwhacker Percussion Tubes (Boomwhackers) Played by being hit on the ground.

Salad Bowls (Wooden or Plastic) Played with hands, sticks, mallets or beaters.

Pots and Pans Turned upside down and played with hands, sticks, mallets or beaters.

Lids for Pots and Pans Placed on a flat surface or kept on the pots and played with wooden or plastic spoons.

Phone Books Played with wooden spoons or mallets.

Empty Cardboard Boxes (for oatmeal, hats, shoes, etc.) Played with hands, sticks, mallets or beaters.

Wastepaper Baskets (Plastic or Rubber) Turned upside down and played with hands, sticks, mallets or beaters.

Empty Coffee Cans Played with hands, sticks, mallets or beaters.

Traditional Instruments

Drums and *accessory* (extra) percussion instruments come in a variety of shapes, types and sizes. It's important to choose an instrument that's just the right size for you, and not one that's too big or too small. Holding your instrument should look and feel comfortable. When you are ready to purchase a drum or percussion accessory, it's a good idea to have your teacher or a music store specialist evaluate whether it is the right size for you.

Below is a partial list of traditional percussion instruments that can be used to produce a variety of sounds. Each instrument is available in a variety of sizes.

Djembe (pronounced **JEM-bay**) A goblet-shaped drum of African origin, the djembe can be played in either a standing position (held with a strap or in a stand), or a sitting position (held with a strap or your leg muscles). It is played with the hands.

Frame Drums Among the oldest instruments in the percussion family, these drums are either round or rectangular and have skin stretched across one or both sides. They are held in one hand and played using the other (with or without a stick or mallet).

Conga Popular in Afro-Cuban drumming, this barrel-shaped drum can be played in either a standing position (held in a stand) or in a sitting position (held with a strap and/or the knees). It is most commonly played with the hands.

Doumbek (pronounced **DOOM-beck**) A goblet-shaped drum found in Egypt, North Africa, and Arabic countries, the doumbek is played with the hands. It can be played resting across your thighs (secured with your arm), or cradled between your legs.

Tambourine A popular instrument for all styles of music, the tambourine consists of metal jingles attached to a shallow wood shell that has a single skin or plastic head. It is held with one hand and shaken, struck or tapped with the other hand.

Bongos This pair of wood-shelled, cylindrical drums are played with the hands in either a standing position (mounted on a stand) or a sitting position (held with the knees).

Maracas and other Shakers These metal, wood, gourd, and plastic containers are filled with beads or pellets. They are held in one or both hands and shaken in an even, back-and-forth motion.

Woodblock This small, rectangular piece of hard wood is shaped to create a resonating chamber. It can be held in the hand, mounted on a woodblock holder, or rested on a padded table and played with drumsticks, hard plastic mallets or hard rubber mallets.

Temple Blocks Two to five hollow, clam- or square-shaped wooden blocks are mounted on a stand and played with drumsticks, yarn mallets and/or medium to hard rubber mallets.

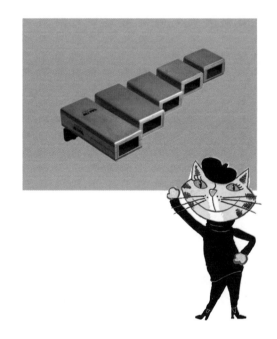

Caring for Your Instrument

Get to know your instrument and treat it like a friend. When you carry it, think of it as part of your body so you don't accidentally bump it against walls or furniture, and be especially careful not to drop it! Every time you're done playing, carefully dust off your instrument with a soft cloth, and be sure to cover it or put it away in its case.

Sticks, Mallets and Beaters

Percussion sound sources are struck with a stick or another object called a *beater*. Below are some traditional types of beaters and some non-traditional, everyday objects that can be used.

Hands

Drumsticks

Mallets made with yarn, rubber or plastic

Pencils with large erasers on the end

Wooden or plastic spoons

Chopsticks, alone or with rubber balls on the ends

Empty paper towel rolls

How to Hold the Sticks, Mallets and Beaters (the Matched Grip)

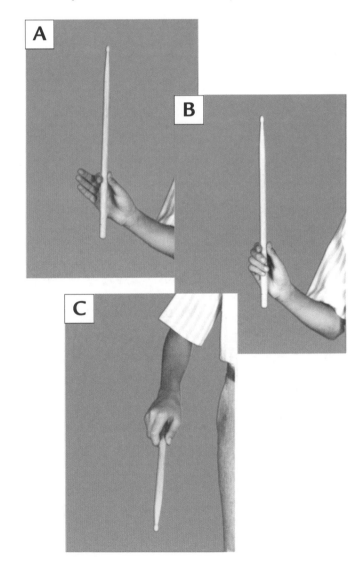

1. First, extend your right hand as if you were going to shake hands with someone.

2. Place the stick or mallet between your thumb and first finger (A).

3. Curve the other fingers around the stick (B).

4. Turn your hand over so your palm is facing towards the floor (C).

5. Repeat steps 1–4 with your left hand.

Beats

To *tap* means to strike the playing surface of your drum or another sound source with your hand, leg, fingers, stick, mallet or other beater to produce a sound.

Each tap you play is equal to one *beat*. Beats are even, like the ticking of a clock.

tick - tick - tick - tick
beat - beat - beat - beat

Body Drumming

Using your body as a sound source to tap out rhythms is called *body drumming*. Your body's "drumset" includes **hand claps**, **foot stomps**, **finger snaps**, **leg pats** (with hands), **chest pats** (with hands) and **head pats** (with hands). Body drumming will help you "feel" the beat and understand the rhythms.

Snap This simple two-finger technique produces a short, high-pitched sound. It is the highest-pitched body sound.

Clap Clapping is not only a means of letting someone know we liked what they did—it can also be used to reinforce the pulse of a song. The clapping sound can be made bright and high by holding your hands flat or by clapping your fingers into your palm. A darker, lower sound can be produced by cupping your hands. Experiment with each of these sounds.

Pat As we listen to music, we pat our thighs when following along with the beat. You can pat your legs faster than you can clap or snap because it's a simple movement that takes only one hand. Patting the legs, head or chest produces a lower pitch sound than clapping.

Stomp Stomping is a good way to feel a steady beat because it is a large body movement. It creates the lowest body percussion sound.

Toe Tap For more control over the volume and accuracy of your beats, keep the heel of your foot on the ground and lift your toes up and down.

Time to Clap and Stomp

 Track 1

The emphasis of the following exercise is on *counting*. Be sure to keep a steady beat.

1. Clap your hands on beats 1, 2, 3 and 4.

Count:	1	2	3	4
	Clap	**Clap**	**Clap**	**Clap**

2. Stomp your right (R) or left (L) foot on beats 1, 2, 3 and 4.
(One-two-three-four, we-are-stomping-on-the-floor!)

Count:	1	2	3	4
	Stomp (R)	**Stomp** (R)	**Stomp** (R)	**Stomp** (R)

Count:	1	2	3	4
	Stomp (L)	**Stomp** (L)	**Stomp** (L)	**Stomp** (L)

Count:	1	2	3	4
	Stomp (R)	**Stomp** (L)	**Stomp** (R)	**Stomp** (L)

3. Clap your hands on beats 1 and 3. Pat your **chest** with your right (R) or left (L) hand on beats 2 and 4.

Count:	1	2	3	4	1	2	3	4
	Clap	**Pat** (R)	**Clap**	**Pat** (L)	**Clap**	**Pat** (R)	**Clap**	**Pat** (L)

4. Stomp your foot on beats 1 and 3. Pat your **head** on beats 2 and 4.

Count:	1	2	3	4	1	2	3	4
	Stomp (R)	**Pat** (R)	**Stomp** (L)	**Pat** (L)	**Stomp** (R)	**Pat** (R)	**Stomp** (L)	**Pat** (L)

Getting Acquainted with Music Notation

Notes

Musical sounds are represented by symbols called *notes*.

Introducing the Quarter Note
(a short note)

stem →

←notehead

1 beat

A black note with a stem is called a *quarter-note*. Each quarter note equals one beat (count "one").

The Staff

A standard *staff* is made up of five lines and the four spaces between those lines. Notes for drum music can be written on a staff with either a single line, a double line, or with five lines.

The Clef

Music for drums is written with a *neutral clef*, also called a *percussion clef*, at the beginning of the staff.

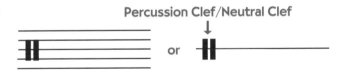

Percussion Clef/Neutral Clef

Bar Lines, Measures, and Time Signatures

Bar lines divide the staff into equal *measures*. A *double bar line* is used to show the end of the music. Measures are always filled with a certain number of beats. You know how many beats are in each measure by looking at the *time signature*, which is always at the beginning of the music after the percussion clef.

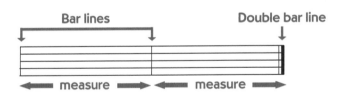

Bar lines

Double bar line

measure

measure

A $\frac{4}{4}$ time signature (called "four-four time") means there are four equal beats in every measure, and a quarter note (♩) gets one beat.

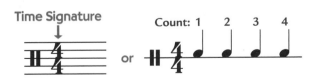

Time Signature

Count: 1 2 3 4

My First Rhythm

General Practice Tips

1. Keep a regular practice schedule.

2. Count out loud and keep a steady beat.

3. Practice the rhythms and exercises slowly at first, then play them along with the CD.

4. Keep a practice diary.

5. Enjoy practicing. Playing drums is fun!

Play this example, which is in $\frac{4}{4}$ time, using any of the sound sources mentioned earlier. Before playing along with the CD, play the exercise at least three times. Remember to keep the beats even and count out loud.

 Track 2

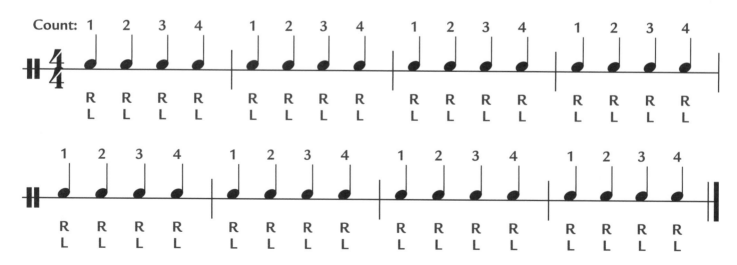

Introducing the Quarter Rest

Rests are signs of silence. This strange-looking music symbol is called a *quarter rest*. It means to be silent for the value of a quarter note (one beat).

1 beat

Rest Warm-up

Before playing "Three Blind Mice," practice this exercise (at least three times) until you are comfortable playing rests. Start slowly, and gradually increase the tempo each time you play.

Track 3

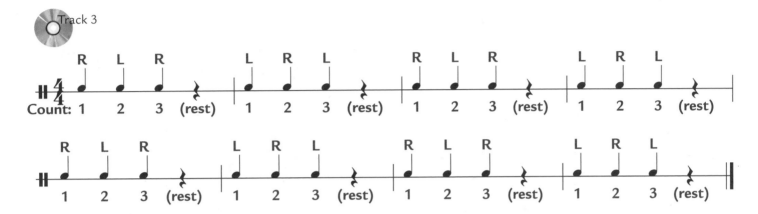

Three Blind Mice

Before playing along with the CD, practice the part alone until you are comfortable with it.

Practice Tip

Tap the rhythms while singing the words.

Track 4

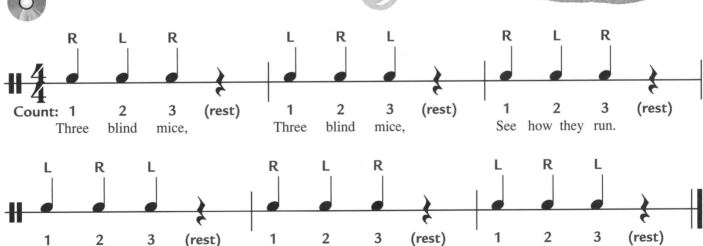

Troubadour Song

Before playing along with the CD, practice the part alone until you are comfortable with it. Start slowly, and gradually increase the tempo. Play this song two times.

Track 5

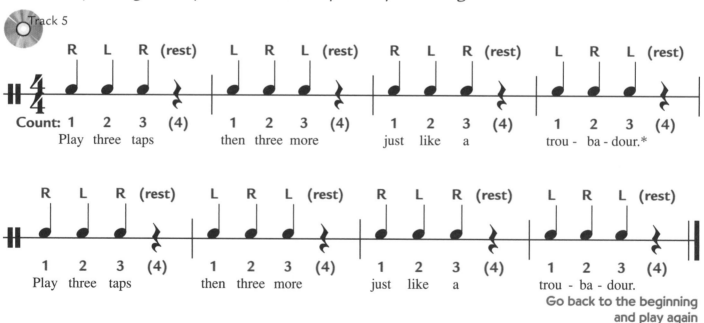

* A *troubadour* was a musician who traveled around singing and playing.

Introducing Two Sound Sources

Track 6

Sound Source No. 1 (top note) =

Sound Source No. 2 (bottom note) =

Play exercises 1–3 using two different sounds sources that you tap with a stick, a mallet, or your hand. Play each exercise at least three times before moving on to the next one. Remember to start slowly and gradually increase the tempo.

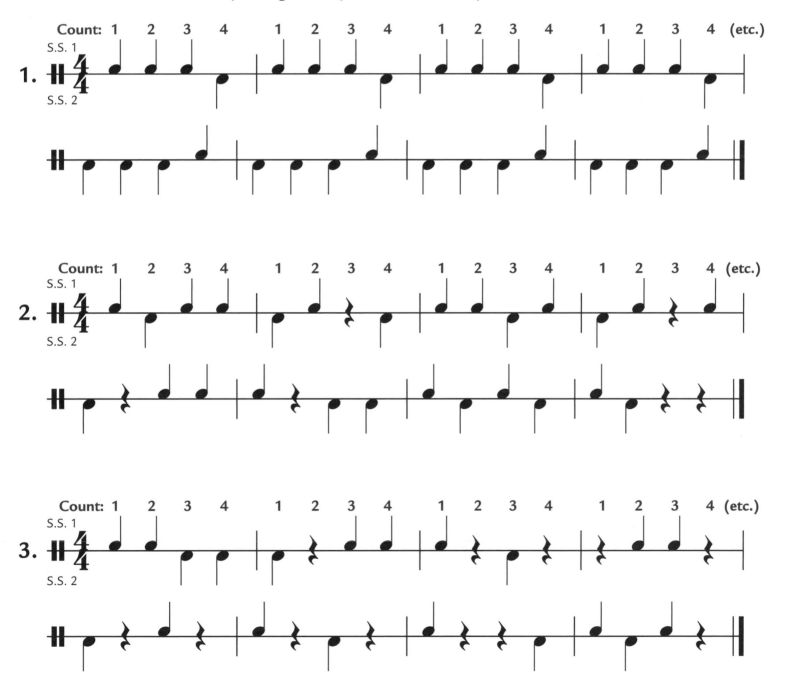

Body Drumming Note = ✗ (one beat)

Play exercise 4 using two of the following sound sources:

- Hand claps
- Foot stomps
- Leg pats
- Head pats
- Chest pats

Start slowly, and gradually increase the tempo.

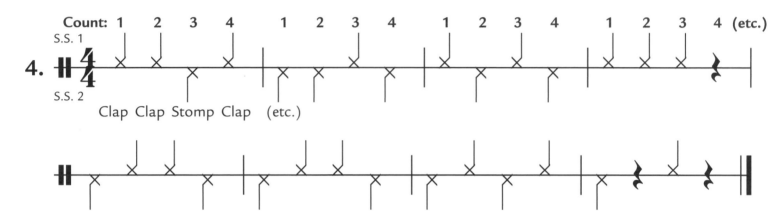

Single Beats, Then Improvise

Before playing along with the CD, practice the part alone until you are comfortable with it. Start slowly, and gradually increase the tempo.

Track 7

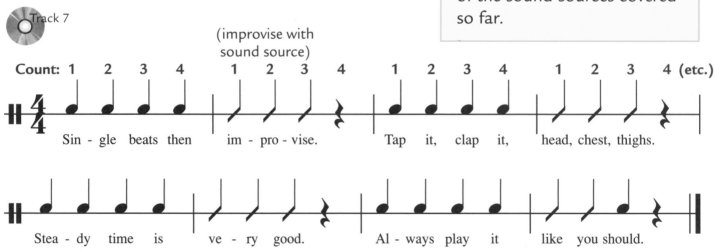

16

Introducing the Half Note
(a long note)

This note lasts two beats (count "one-two" or "half-note"). A half note is twice as long as a quarter note.

2 beats

For the following exercises, use your hand or stick to make large circles on your drum or sound source to match the number of beats for each half note.

Track 8

Tap and Count out Loud

Introducing the Half Rest

This music symbol means do not play for the value of a half note.

A half rest is the same as two quarter rests.

Track 9

Tap and Count out Loud

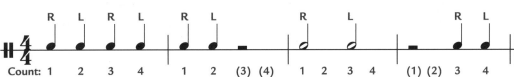

Introducing the Whole Note
(a very long note)

This note lasts four beats (count "one-two-three-four"). A whole note is as long as two half notes or four quarter notes.

4 beats

For the following exercise, use your hand or stick to make large circles on your drum or sound source to match the number of beats for each half note or whole note.

Track 10

Tap and Count out Loud

17

Introducing the Eighth Note

This note looks like a quarter note with a *flag* added to its stem (♪).

Two or more eighth notes are joined together by a *beam* (♫).

An eighth note receives one half beat in $\frac{4}{4}$ time.

Two eighth notes are played in the time of one quarter note (count "one-and").

Count: 1 & 2 &

Skip to My Lou

Before playing along with the CD, practice the part alone until you are comfortable with it. Start slowly, and gradually increase the tempo. Play this song two times.

Track 11

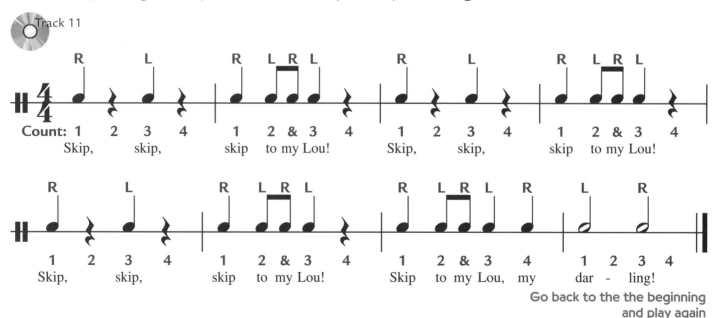

Go back to the the beginning
and play again

18

Introducing Repeat Dots :|

Double dots on the inside of a double bar line mean to go back to the beginning and play again.

Merrily We Roll Along

Track 12

(improvise)   (improvise)

1. Mer- ri - ly we roll a - long, roll a - long, roll a - long.

(improvise)   (improvise)   **Repeat from the beginning**

Mer- ri - ly— we roll a - long— o'er the— deep blue sea.—

Body Drumming

Play the following part using two different sound sources (hands, feet, etc.). Before playing along with the CD, practice the part alone until you are comfortable with it (at least three times). Start slowly, and gradually increase the tempo. Once you've mastered it, go back and play it along with track 12.

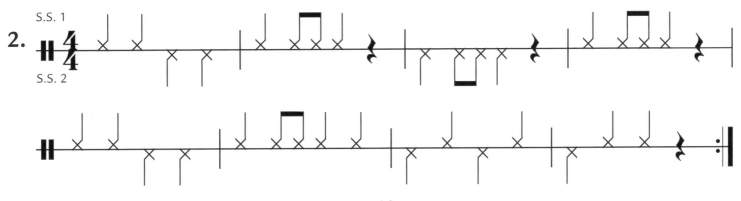

S.S. 1

2.

S.S. 2

19

London Bridge

Before playing along with the CD, practice each part alone until you are comfortable with it. Start slowly, and gradually increase the tempo.

Track 13

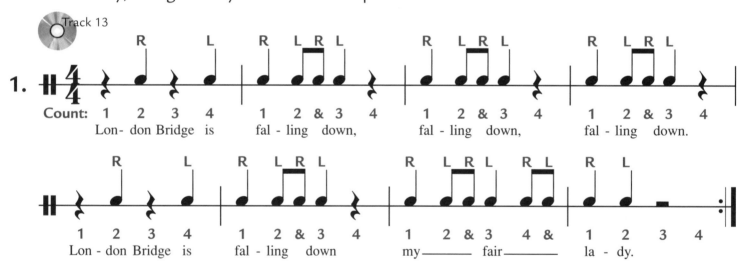

Body Drumming

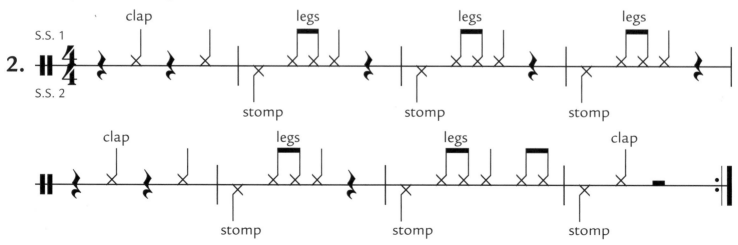

Introducing $\frac{2}{4}$ Time

2 means there are two beats in each measure.

4 means a quarter note (♩) gets one beat.

$\frac{2}{4}$ Time Warm-up

Play the following exercise at least three times. Remember to practice slowly at first, then gradually increase the tempo.

Track 14

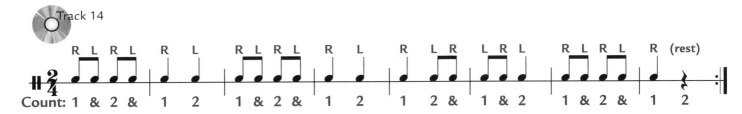

The Double Stroke

Up until this point, you have been alternating your hands and feet (L–R or R–L). In the following exercises, you will play two strokes in a row with each hand (R–R or L–L). This is called a *double stroke*.

Play each exercise at least three times before moving on to the next one. Start slowly, and gradually increase the tempo.

Track 14

21

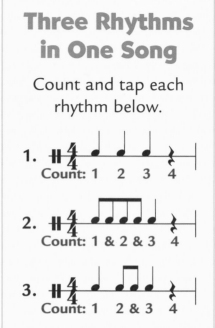
Rain Comes Down Track 15

Before playing along with the CD, practice the part alone until you are comfortable with it. Start slowly, and gradually increase the tempo.

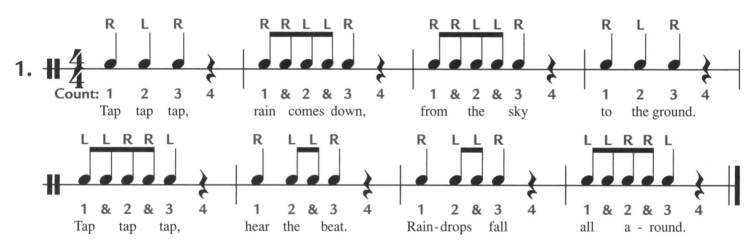

```
      R   L   R          R R L L R          R R L L R          R   L   R
1. 4/4
   Count: 1  2  3  4      1 & 2 & 3  4      1 & 2 & 3  4      1   2   3  4
         Tap tap tap,    rain comes down,  from the sky      to the ground.

      L L R R L          R   L L R          R   L L R          L L R R L
      1 & 2 & 3  4       1   2 & 3  4       1   2 & 3  4       1 & 2 & 3  4
      Tap  tap tap,     hear the beat.    Rain-drops fall    all  a - round.
```

Improvise on a Sound Source

Repeat the following exercises at least three times.
Start slowly, and gradually increase the tempo.

2. 4/4

Body Drumming

H = Head pat   C = Chest pat   L = Leg pat

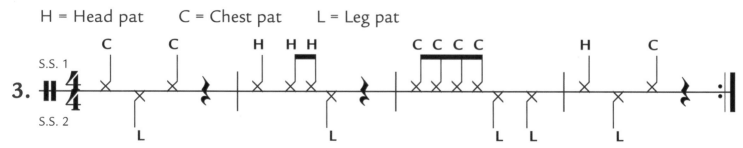

3. 4/4

S.S. 1

S.S. 2

Introducing Coordination

Playing Two Rhythms on Different Sound Sources at the Same Time

Can you rub your belly with your left hand while you pat your head with your right hand? Good! Now switch hands, and rub your belly with your right hand while patting your head with your left hand. The ability to do this is called *coordination*. Once this becomes comfortable, you should be able to play two rhythms on different sound sources at the same time, as in the following exercises.

Play each exercise at least three times before moving on to the next one. Start slowly, and gradually increase the tempo.

1.
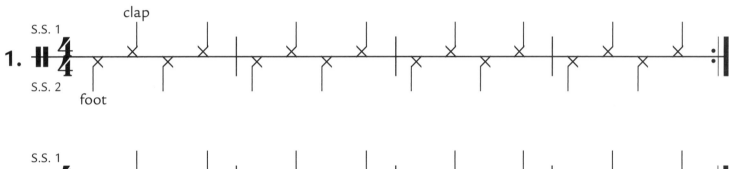

2.
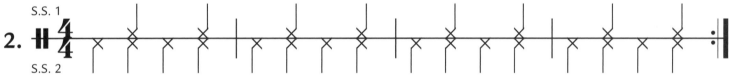

3.

4.
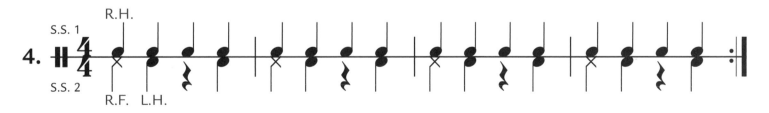

5.
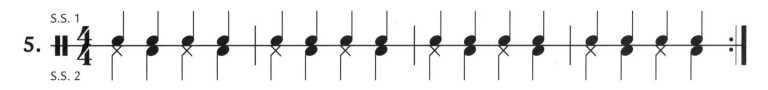

Love Somebody

Before playing along with the CD, practice each part alone until you are comfortable with it. Start slowly, and gradually increase the tempo. Once you've mastered part 1 and can comfortably play it with track 16 on the CD, go back and play part 2 along with the same track.

Track 16

Love some - bod - y, yes I —— do! Love some - bod - y, won't — say who.

Love some - bod - y, can you — guess? Who's the one that I love best?

Alternate Part

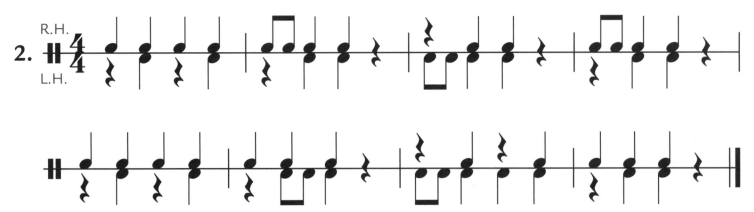

More Advanced Coordination

Play the following exercises along with track 17. Repeat the first exercise at least three times before moving on to the second exercise.

Introducing Dotted Notes

A dot (.) placed after a note increases the note's length by one-half the original value.

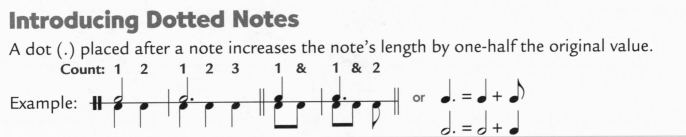

Play each exercise at least three times before moving on to the next exercise.
Remember to start slowly and gradually increase the tempo.

A Brief History of Dixieland

In the early 1900s, jazz music started taking on a unique sound and form, especially in the city of New Orleans, Louisiana. Brass bands, gospel music, folk dances, the work songs of enslaved Africans, and the *syncopation** of ragtime music all played important roles in the development of this unique style called Dixieland.

*See page 45 for definition.

Introducing the Accent >

This symbol means to play the note a little louder.

When the Saints Go Marching In

This tune is considered to be the theme song of Dixieland. It is usually played at the end of a performance as a grand finale.

Before playing along with the CD, practice the part alone until you are comfortable with it. Start slowly, and gradually increase the tempo. Remember to play the accented notes a little louder.

Track 18

*Play this note the second time only.

Jumping Around

Use three different sound sources in this song. Before playing along with the CD, practice the part alone until you are comfortable with it. Start slowly, and gradually increase the tempo.

Track 19

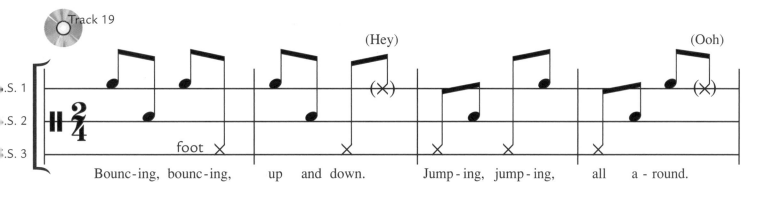

Bounc-ing, bounc-ing, up and down. Jump-ing, jump-ing, all a-round.

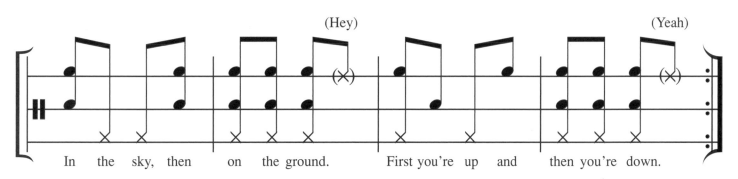

In the sky, then on the ground. First you're up and then you're down.

Yankee Doodle

A fife is a short, hollow flute usually made from a single piece of wood, having generally six finger holes and sometimes one or more keys. Fifes and drums have been around for centuries. Military fifers and drummers were usually used to help direct the *cadence* (the beat of rhythmic movement) of a march, for roll call, and to signal soldiers into battle.

Before playing along with the CD, practice the drum part alone until you are comfortable with it. Start slowly, and gradually increase the tempo. Remember to play the accented notes a little louder.

Measure Repeat Sign   𝄍

This sign tells you to repeat the previous measure.

Track 20

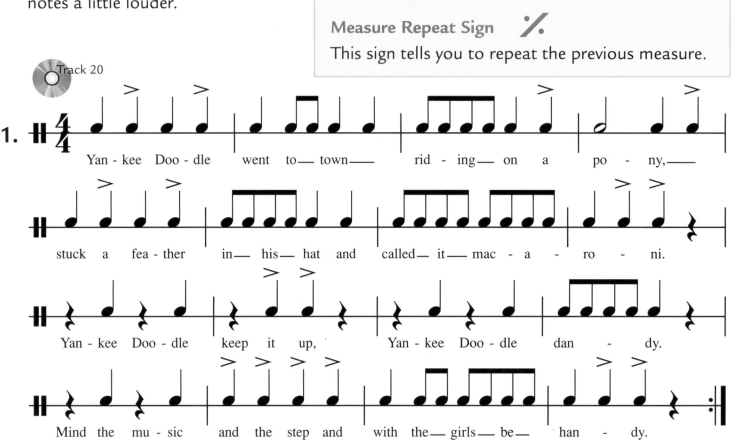

1.

Yan - kee Doo - dle   went to— town——   rid - ing— on a   po - ny,——

stuck a fea - ther   in— his— hat and   called— it— mac - a - ro - ni.

Yan - kee Doo - dle   keep it up,   Yan - kee Doo - dle   dan - dy.

Mind the mu - sic   and the step and   with the— girls— be— han - dy.

Body Drumming

Practice the following part at least three times before going back and playing it along with track 20. Start slowly, and gradually increase the tempo. Play this song two times.

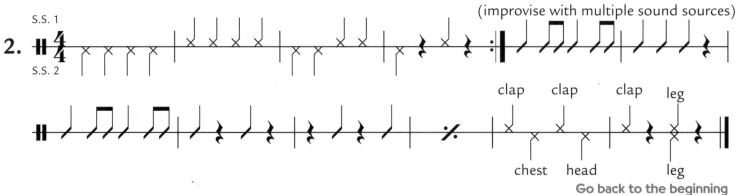

S.S. 1

2.

S.S. 2

(improvise with multiple sound sources)

clap   clap   clap   leg

chest   head   leg

Go back to the beginning
and play again

28

Introducing Singles and Doubles

When you play single strokes and double strokes together, both a sound pattern and a sticking pattern are created. One of these sticking patterns has a funny name called a *paradiddle,* which is one of the most common drum rudiments.

Elizabeth, the Elephant

A pickup note is a note that precedes (comes in front of) the first full measure. The first note of this song is a pickup note. Remember to count, and start on the "&" of beat 2. Before playing along with the CD, practice the part alone until you are comfortable with it. Start slowly, and gradually increase the tempo.

Track 21

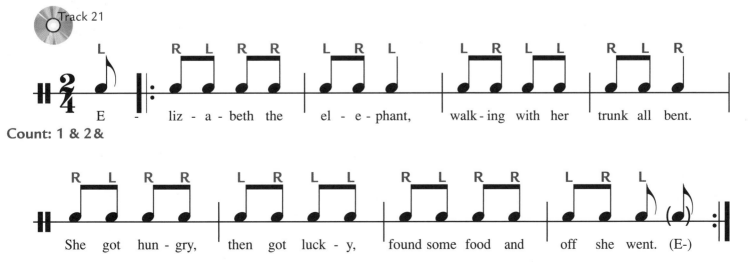

29

Paradiddle Exercises

Play each of the following exercises at least three times before moving on to the next one. Start slowly, and gradually increase the tempo.

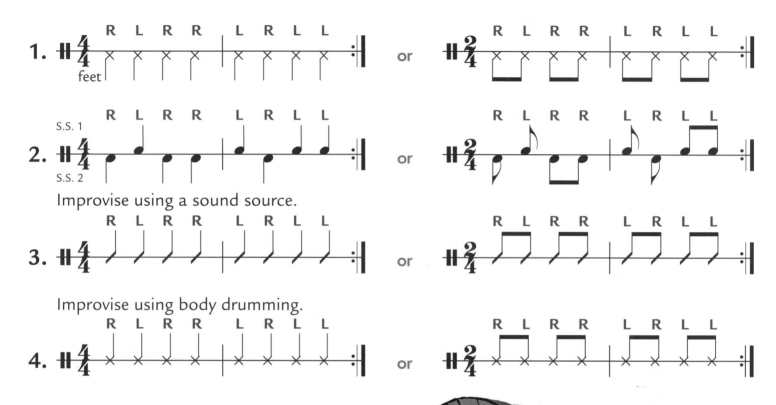

Improvise using a sound source.

Improvise using body drumming.

Brave in the Cave

Before playing along with the CD, practice the part alone until you are comfortable with it. Start slowly, and gradually increase the tempo.

Track 22

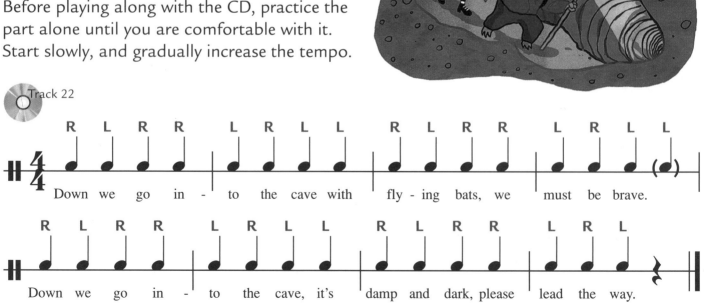

Introducing the Sixteenth Note

This note looks like an eighth note with an additional flag added to its stem (♬).

Two or more sixteenth notes are joined together by a *double beam* (♬♬).

Four sixteenth notes are played in the time of one quarter note (♬♬ = ♩).

1 e & a

salt and pep-per

Before playing along with the CD, repeat each exercise at least three times before moving on to the next one.

Track 23

Call: Response: - - - - - - ⌐

Count: 1   2 &   1 e & a 2

Call: Response: - - - - - - ⌐

Count: 1 e & a 2 e & a   1 & 2

Up-Down-Up

Before playing along with the CD, practice each part alone until you are comfortable with it. Start slowly, and gradually increase the tempo.

Track 24

1. S.S. 1 / S.S. 2   Up - down - up   up - down - up   up———down———   up - down - up

2. S.S. 1 / S.S. 2   high   low

Body Drumming

chest   clap   top of head   clap

3. S.S. 1 / S.S. 2   legs   stomp   chest

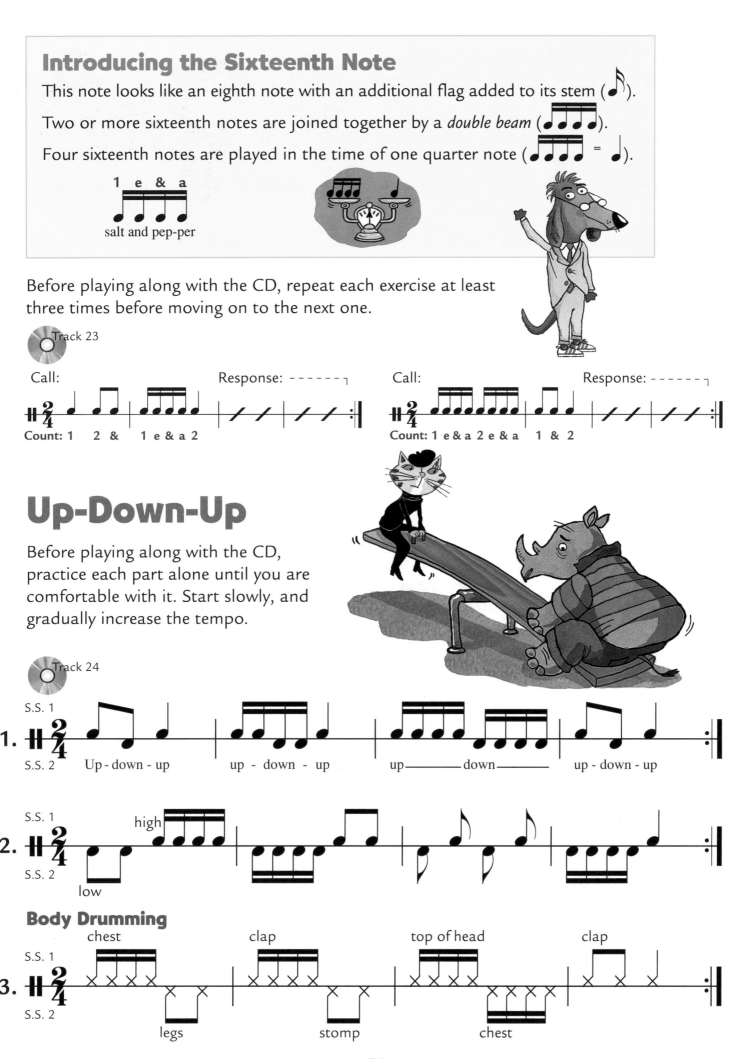

31

Trio (Up-Down-Up)

A *trio* is a musical composition for three voices (singers) or instruments (players).

Before playing along with the CD, practice each part alone until you are comfortable with it. Start slowly, and gradually increase the tempo.

 Track 24

1.

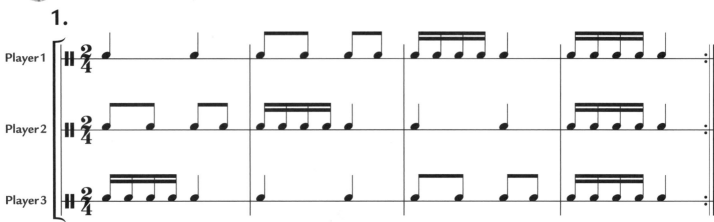

2.

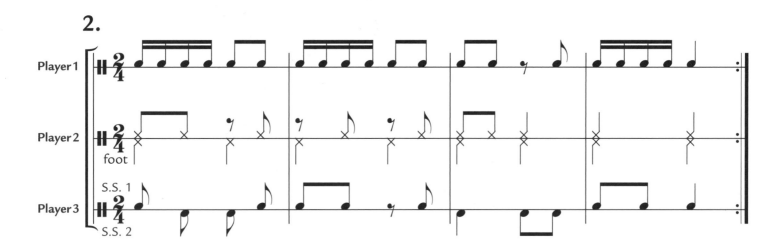

3. Body Drumming

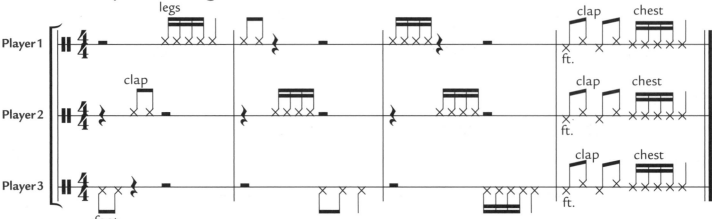

32

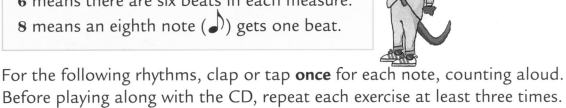

Introducing $\frac{6}{8}$ Time

6 means there are six beats in each measure.

8 means an eighth note ($\eighthnote$) gets one beat.

Track 25

For the following rhythms, clap or tap **once** for each note, counting aloud. Before playing along with the CD, repeat each exercise at least three times.

Dotted quarter note ($\dottedquarter$)
or rests ($\quarterrest$ $\eighthrest$) = 3 beats
(Count: 1 2 3)

Quarter note ($\quarternote$)
or quarter rest ($\quarterrest$) = 2 beats
(Count: 1 2)

Eighth note ($\eighthnote$)
or eighth rest ($\eighthrest$) = 1 beat
(Count: 1)

1. Call: ... Response: ...
Count: 1 2 3 4 5 6 1 2 3 4 5 6

2. Call: ... Response: ...
Count: 1 2 3 4 5 6 1 2 3 4 5 6

3. Call: ... Response: ...
Count: 1 2 3 4 5 6 1 2 3 4 5 6

Track 26

La Raspa
(A Mexican Stomping or Hat Dance)

Before playing along with the CD, practice the part alone until you are comfortable with it. Start slowly, and gradually increase the tempo.

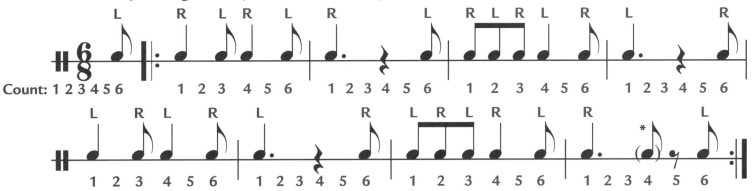

Count: 1 2 3 4 5 6   1 2 3 4 5 6   1 2 3 4 5 6   1 2 3 4 5 6   1 2 3 4 5 6

1 2 3 4 5 6   1 2 3 4 5 6   1 2 3 4 5 6   1 2 3 4 5 6

*Play this note the second time only!

33

The Mountain Climber

Track 27

Before playing along with the CD, practice the part alone until you are comfortable with it. Start slowly, and gradually increase the tempo.

1.

The fear-less climb - er, gear from head to toe,

climbs the moun - tain toward the peaks of snow.

Play four times.

2.

R.F. L.F. (etc.)

Itsy Bitsy Spider

Before playing along with the CD, practice the part alone until you are comfortable with it. Start slowly, and gradually increase the tempo.

Track 28

Body Drumming

S.S. 1

Count: 1 2 3 4 5 6

S.S. 2 The it - sy, bit - sy spi - der, climbed up the wa - ter spout. Down came the rain and

washed the spi - der out. Out came the sun and dried up all the

rain, so the it - sy, bit - sy spi - der climbed up the spout a - gain.

34

Mary Had a Little Lamb

Track 29

Before playing along with the CD, practice each version alone until you are comfortable with it. Start slowly, and gradually increase the tempo. Make sure you watch the music!

Two-Beat Variation Play eight times.

Track 30

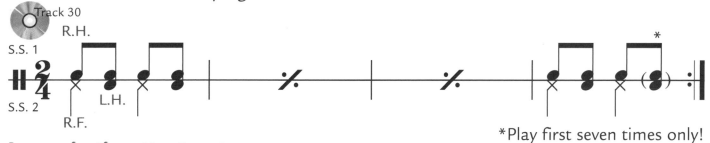

*Play first seven times only!

Improvisation Play four times.

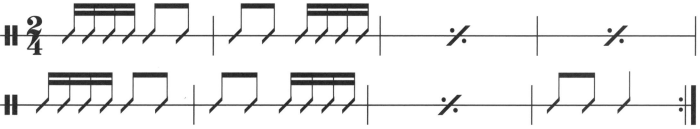

35

Introducing the Duet

A *duet* is a musical composition for two voices (singers) or instruments (players).

Ping Pong Song

Before playing along with the CD, practice the part alone until you are comfortable with it. Start slowly, and gradually increase the tempo.

Track 31

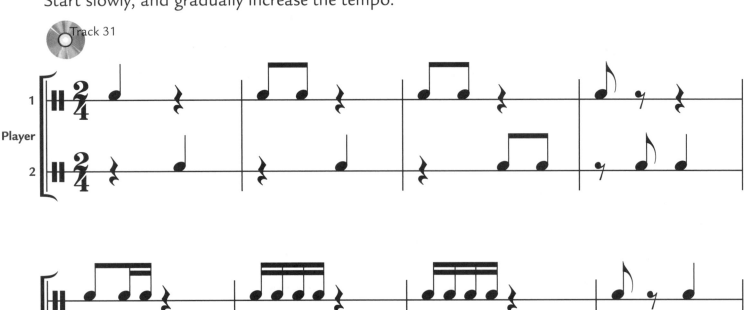

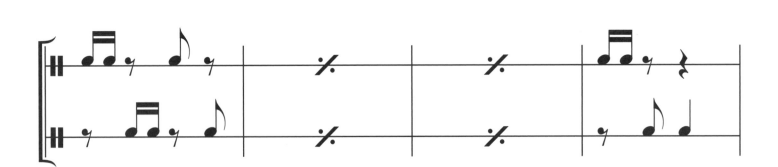

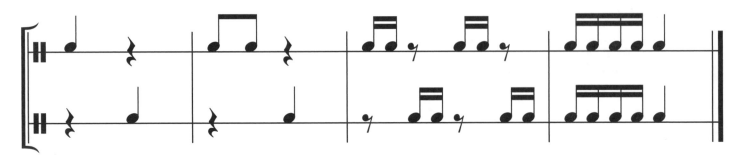

36

Soccer Game

Before playing along with the CD, practice the part alone until you are comfortable with it. Start slowly, and gradually increase the tempo.

Track 32

Play four times.

Pass it!   Steal it!

Kick it!   Score

Trio

Play four times.

Player 1   low sound

Player 2   clap

Player 3   foot stomp

Pumpkin Song

Introducing Two New Rhythms

Count and tap each rhythm below.

1. $\frac{2}{4}$ Count: 1 e & 2 &

2. $\frac{2}{4}$ Count: 1 & a 2 &

Track 33

Before playing along with the CD, practice each part alone until you are comfortable with it. Start slowly, and gradually increase the tempo.

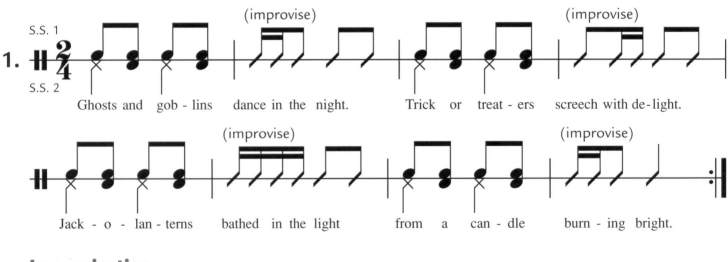

S.S. 1
1.
S.S. 2

(improvise)   (improvise)

Ghosts and gob-lins   dance in the night.   Trick or treat-ers   screech with de-light.

(improvise)   (improvise)

Jack-o-lan-terns   bathed in the light   from a can-dle   burn-ing bright.

Improvisation

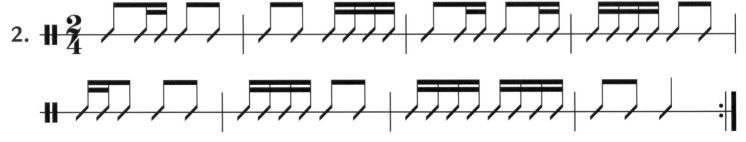

2.

38

Ode to Joy
(from Beethoven's 9th Symphony)

Before playing along with the CD, practice each part alone until you are comfortable with it. Start slowly, and gradually increase the tempo.

Track 34

Rock Beat

Improvisation

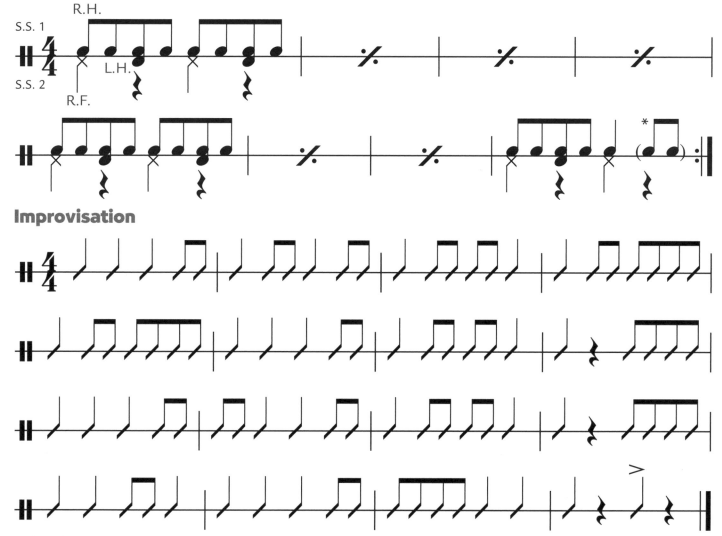

*Play first time only!

A-Choo!

Track 35

Before playing along with the CD, practice each part alone until you are comfortable with it. Start slowly, and gradually increase the tempo. Play four times.

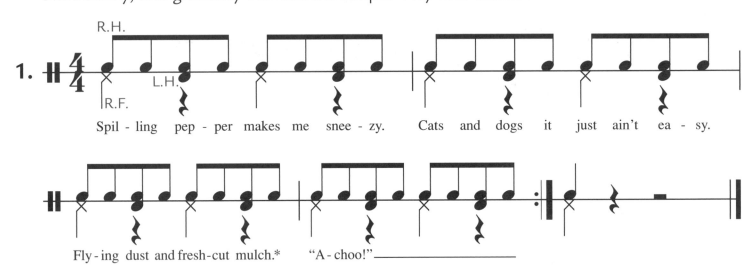

1.

Spil - ling pep – per makes me snee - zy. Cats and dogs it just ain't ea - sy.

Fly - ing dust and fresh-cut mulch.* "A - choo!"

Play four times.

2.

(improvise)

Body Drumming
Play four times.

3.

clap   legs   chest   (improvise)   clap

S.S. 1

S.S. 2

(run in place with feet)

Mulch is a ground covering made of cut grass or sawdust.

40

Jingle Bells

Track 36

Before playing along with the CD, practice each part alone until you are comfortable with it. Start slowly, and gradually increase the tempo.

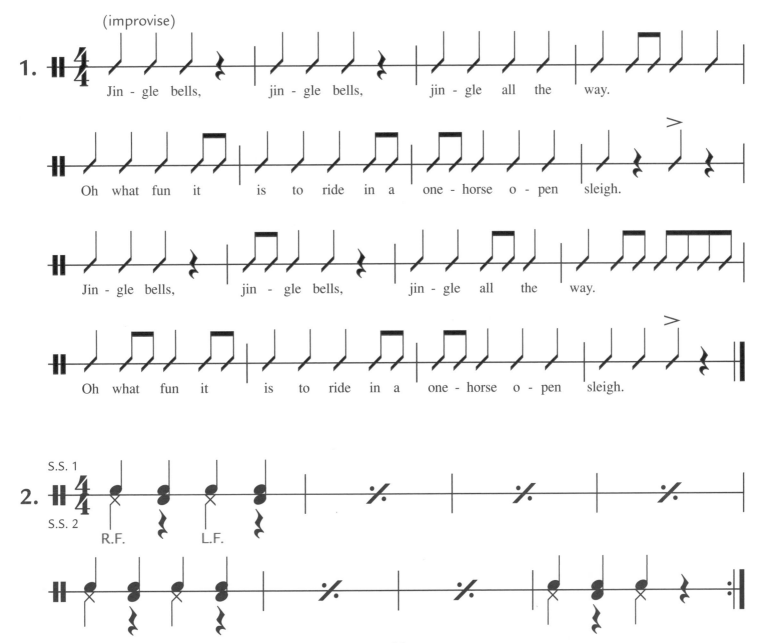

Alouette

Use different sound sources to improvise rhythms within the rests. Before playing along with the CD, practice the part alone until you are comfortable with it. Start slowly, and gradually increase the tempo.

Track 37

Introducing Jazz

Jazz is a style of music that was created in the United States. What makes jazz sound like jazz?

1. The melody is often *embellished* (has added details), *syncopated* (see page 45 for definition), or *varied* at the performer's discretion.

2. The harmony may include more *dissonant* (clashing) notes.

3. The rhythm emphasizes beats 2 and 4, which gives it a "swing" feel.

4. Jazz musicians compose new melodies on the spot, which is called *improvisation*.

Taking a Walk

Before playing along with the CD, practice each part alone until you are comfortable with it. Start slowly, and gradually increase the tempo.

Track 38

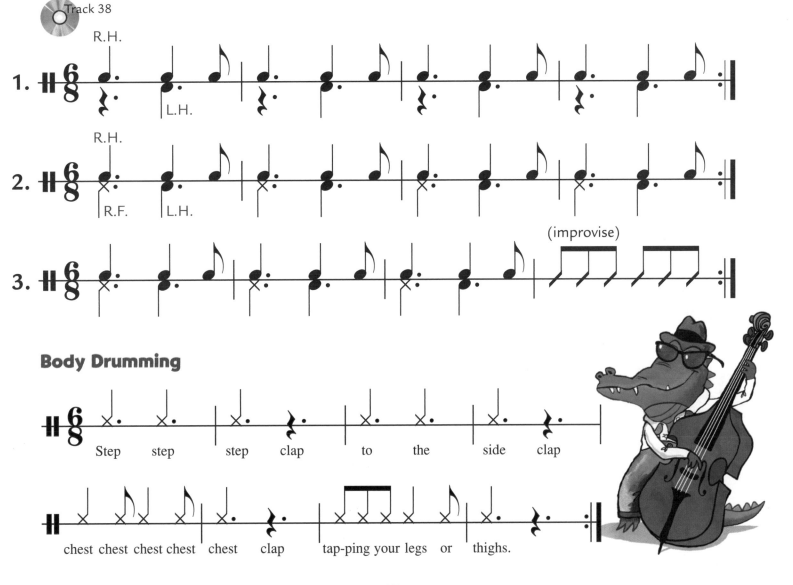

Little Steps and Big Leaps

 Track 39

Before playing along with the CD, practice each part alone until you are comfortable with it. Start slowly, and gradually increase the tempo.

Play the first line seven times.

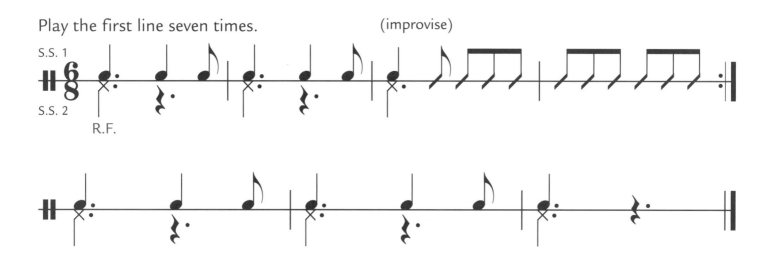

Body Drumming

Play the first line seven times.

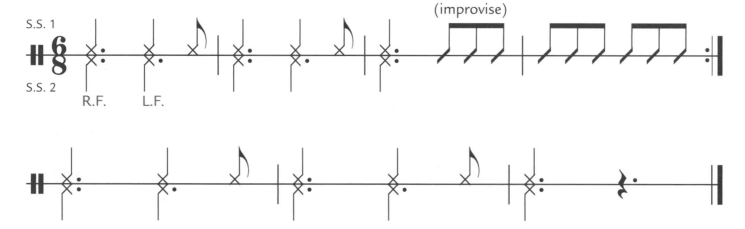

Introducing Syncopation

Notes that are played between the main beats of a measure and held across the beat are called *syncopated* notes. In the following rhythm, the first quarter note is syncopated.

Count: 1 & 2 & 3 & 4 &

Syncopation also occurs when a note that is one beat or longer starts on an "&".

Count: 1 & 2 & 3 & 4 &

Before playing along with the CD, practice the following rhythms separately until you are comfortable with them. Start slowly, and gradually increase the tempo.

Swing (a Style of Jazz)

Track 40

1.

Count: 1 & 2 & 3 4   1 & 2 & 3 4   1 2 3 & 4 &   1 & 2 & 3 4

Taiko (a Japanese Style of Drumming)

Track 41

2.

Count: 1 2 3 & 4 &   1 2 3 & 4 &   1 2 3 & 4 &   1 & a 2 & 3 4

Tango (a Latin-American Dance)

Track 42

3.

Count: 1 & 2 & 3 4   1 2 & 3 4   1 & 2 & 3 4   1 & 2 & 3 4

1 & 2 & 3 4   1 & 2 & 3 4   1 2 3 & 4 &   1 2 & 3 4

45

Aura Lee

Before playing along with the CD, practice each part alone until you are comfortable with it. Start slowly, and gradually increase the tempo.

Track 43

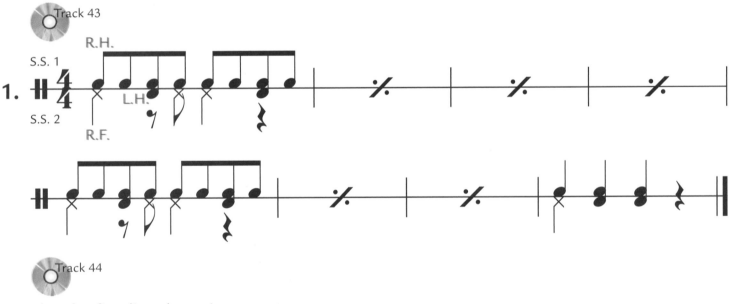

Track 44

Play the first line three times.

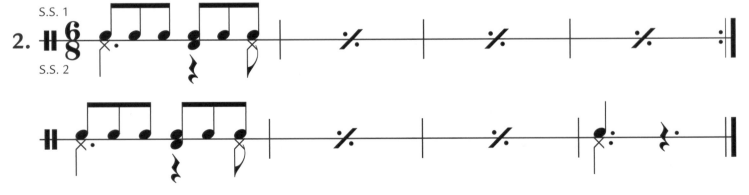

She'll Be Comin' 'Round the Mountain

Before playing along with the CD, practice each part alone until you are comfortable with it. Start slowly, and gradually increase the tempo.

Track 45

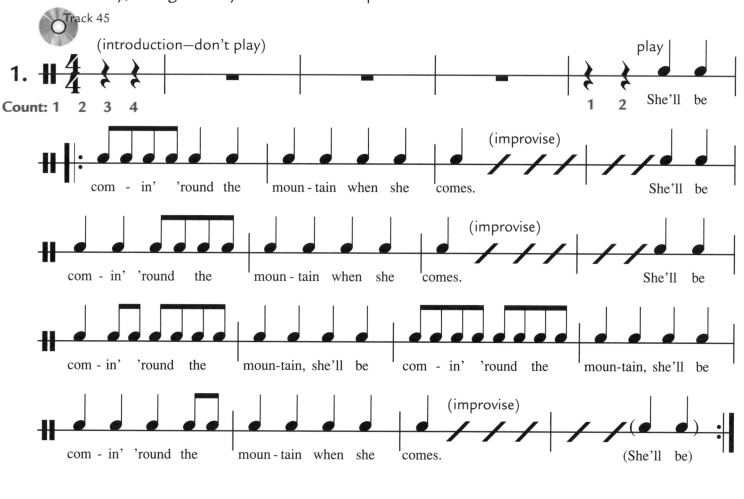

Body Drumming

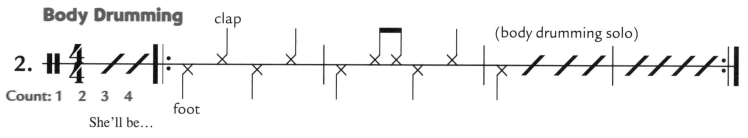

Certificate of Promotion

This certifies that

_____

has mastered and perfected

Book 1 of Alfred's Kid's Drum Course

and is hereby promoted into

Book 2 of Alfred's Kid's Drum Course.

_____   _____
Teacher / Parent   Date